Это 18

RUSSIAN

Dette er 18

NORWEGIAN

Das ist 18

GERMAN

Hii Ni 18

SWAHILI

זה 18

HEBREW

این 18 است

FARSI

The New York Times
Amulet Books · New York

This
Is
18

EDITED BY
Jessica Bennett

WITH
Sandra Stevenson,
Sharon Attia,
AND Anya Strzemien

18

Editor's note: The following interviews were conducted in 2018 and 2019. As such, the ages of subjects and photographers reflect the time at which the interviews were conducted.

ISBN 978-1-4197-4123-4

Book design by Andrew Teoh and Sebit Min

Printed and bound in USA

10 9 8 7 6 5 4 3 2 1

Amulet Books are available at special discounts when purchased in quantity for premiums and promotions as well as fundraising or educational use. Special editions can also be created to specification. For details, contact specialsales@abramsbooks.com or the address below.

ABRAMS The Art of Books
195 Broadway, New York, NY 10007
abramsbooks.com

To girls everywhere and the strong women they will become

Introduction

When Malala Yousafzai turned 18, she opened a school for Syrian refugee girls, calling on leaders from around the world to provide "books, not bullets."

It was at 18 that Cleopatra became ruler of Egypt in 51 BCE and Victoria the queen of Great Britain in 1837, over which she would reign for nearly 64 years.

Serena Williams had won the U.S. Open by the time she was 18, and Emma González had become a global leader in the movement to end gun violence.

I was doing nothing nearly so noble or successful at 18.

I was finishing up high school in Seattle, cutting class to eat Wendy's Frosties with my girlfriends, and working at a restaurant on the weekends. I don't remember feeling particularly *adult*—I was still living under my parents' roof, abiding by their rules and extremely annoying curfews—but I do remember feeling like my life was about to change.

I would soon vote for the first time, in an election that taught me that "hanging chads" were not just annoying guys named Chad who were always hanging around. I would go away to college, managing to road trip through three states with only one speeding ticket (and a near-accident my parents still don't know about). I would sign a lease on my first apartment—though my parents paid the deposit—and eventually get my first credit card. (Sidenote: Did you know that women couldn't get credit cards in their own names until the 1970s?)

A year later, Britney Spears's "I'm Not a Girl, Not Yet a Woman" would come out—she, by the way, had two No. 1

albums on the *Billboard* chart by the time she was 18—
and, you know, I *felt her*. I could buy cigarettes if I wanted!
But just please don't tell my mom and dad. (They were
still traumatized by my belly button piercing.)

Eighteen is an age, yes. But it's also something more.
It's a rite of passage. It's a pathway. It's a time to savor the
last carefree moments of adolescence—and it's a gateway
into being an adult.

It is all of these things to 18-year-olds of any gender,
but it is particularly significant for girls. Around the world,
1 in 5 girls will be married by that age. There are more
than 100 million girls under 18 who are not in school.
In the United States, girls' confidence falls dramatically
during the years just before 18, and globally, girls are less
likely than boys to say they feel happy with their lives.

Girls are also less likely to be portrayed in mainstream
media, and are often depicted as one-dimensional
characters when they are. Part of that has to do with who
has historically been behind the camera. Women make
up a fraction of professional photographers and creative
directors, and in film and on television, girls are less
likely to speak on camera—and more likely to be shown
without their clothes on.

For those reasons and more, when my colleagues and
I set out to document the lives of 18-year-old girls around
the world—and a few soon-to-be 18-year-olds—we didn't
want to hire professional photojournalists. We wanted
other girls to do the capturing. Who better to document
the lives of teenagers than other teens?

So we went about finding young women photographers and asked *them* to tell us the stories of 18-year-old girls in their communities. In the following pages, you'll meet 18-year-old girls from 23 cities across 6 continents and 12 time zones, speaking 15 different languages.

You'll spend time with Mahak, a young Indian woman who is a classical dancer and wants to become a teacher, and Liana, one of the few women in Iran who play the bagpipe and who recently performed in an all-women show.

You'll get to know Millie, who works in a pub in Melbourne and is part of an all-girls skate crew, and Rawnaa, from Saudi Arabia, who works as a part-time barista and dreams of learning to drive. (Women in Saudi Arabia were only recently granted that right, and some of the early activists who fought for it were arrested and remain in jail.)

We'll introduce you to Grace, a transgender activist and filmmaker in upstate New York, and Madison, a new mom in Mississippi.

These girls are (literally) a world away from one another, and yet many of them have similar interests. Nearly half say they worry about global warming. Almost all have hopes and dreams of changing the world for the better. They care about politics and social justice and use slang words like "peng" and "dope." They find solace in their bedrooms—what Grace calls "my temple." Many of them still go to their moms for advice.

And they love—like, really love—their phones, though they also worry that their generation spends too much time on them.

We began this project knowing that we wanted to capture life in wildly different locations and circumstances from each other—and from our own. What we found were differences, yes, but also ties that bind. These girls left us reflecting on the young women we used to be and the women we are still becoming.

I thought Hélène, an art student in Los Angeles, captured the contradiction—and beauty—of this moment perfectly when she said: "Eighteen is that little gray spot between adulthood and childhood. You're still a little kid, but the world is like, 'You're a grown-up,' and you somehow have to merge the two."

I'm thrilled to bring you *This Is 18*—a look at girls' lives through girls' eyes.

—Jessica Bennett, Editor

CONTENTS

Shenzhi Xu
Chengdu, China

Shenzhi is a first-year college student majoring in English.

PHOTOGRAPHED BY Luxi Yang

What's something you'd like to learn?
I want to learn many things, but if I had to pick one, I'd want to learn tae kwon do.

For self-defense?
No, it's just cool.

What's a place you've never been to but would like to go?
Russia. I've always thought Russia is a mysterious country, so I've always wanted to go.

Who do you go to for advice?
I usually solve problems on my own. If I really can't solve something, I go to my peers or to a trusted elder.

"Honestly, I don't think that age is the true indicator of whether a person is an adult or not; even when I turn 18, I don't automatically cross into the world of an adult."

If you could have dinner with anyone, who would it be?
Zeyan Li. He is actually a character in a video game.

What is he like?
He is exactly what I would look for in my future spouse, in terms of both personality and appearance. He's quite mature, reserved, prudent, but also very pure.

Shenzhi takes a selfie at a coffee shop.

Shenzhi at karaoke
with friends.

**Do you think a person like that exists in
real life?**
No. Because in the video game, his mind is
not contaminated by reality. He is very pure—
especially when it comes to romance. I think a
person like that wouldn't exist. It is impossible to
find a perfect person.

**What are you looking forward to about
being 18?**
Honestly, I don't think that age is the true
indicator of whether a person is an adult or
not. Even when I turn 18, I don't automatically
cross into the world of an adult. When I turn
18, though, I'll enter college, and that'll be the
first time I experience living on my own. I'll
have more freedom to do what I want with my
time, and I'll develop my own habits and build a
new social circle. I'm very excited. Freedom and
independence are very important to me.

Shenzi in her school classroom.

Meet the Photographer

LUXI YANG

18
Chengdu,
CHINA

When Luxi's not taking photos:
"I'm either watching movies, going on Instagram, or reading books."

Something most people don't know about her:
"I'm really into Chinese rock music from the '90s."

"Chocolate milk with toast and fried eggs."

–Thalia, CUBA

"I eat a McMuffin—a sandwich with eggs, cheese, and bacon."

–Lori'anne, CANADA

What's for Breakfast?

"This is more than usual because it's Shabbat, and on Shabbat morning the whole family eats together."

–Lior, ISRAEL

"My mom's homemade bread with cheese, paprika, and a glass of milk."

—Rena, NORWAY

"Oatmeal with brown sugar and cinnamon, rose tea, tater tots, and a banana from my school's cafeteria."

—Hélène, CALIFORNIA

"I love breakfast, especially what we call cornflakes and milk, because it doesn't take much to prepare. You simply need to place cornflakes in the bowl, add milk and sugar. You can choose to have cold milk or boiled milk. Either way, it tastes good."

—Wanjiku, KENYA

"Weetabix with berries."

—Ruby, U.K.

"White rice and beef stew."

—Victory, NIGERIA

Millie Landewee
Melbourne, Australia

Millie is part of an all-girls skate crew called DNL. It stands for "Did Not Land," a joke about not landing tricks. At night she works as a bartender.

PHOTOGRAPHED BY Eremaya Albrecht

Millie at a comic book store.

How do you get around?
Trains mostly. I love trains. It takes me about 40 minutes to get into the city, and it gives me a long time to think.

What do you do when you feel bored?
I work on my comic book, which is exciting. I'm going to spend a couple of months on it, or as much time as I need to finish it, and then I'm going to throw a party when it's done. I'm going to get it properly printed and everything.

What's your favorite spot inside your home?
My bedroom.

And outside?
I like my back deck, the sun just comes through so nicely. And it has plants everywhere. It's really nice.

What's one thing you don't know that you'd like to learn?
I want to learn another language. French is the big one. I really like French.

Millie in her bedroom.

At the skate park
with friends.

What worries you about the future?
This is such a big question. Honestly, we have environmental issues. There is racial stereotyping. I worry about women's rights and women's safety. The fact that one woman a week is murdered by her current or past partner in Australia—and that all my friends are so afraid to walk home alone—this really worries me.

Where do you see yourself in 5 years?
I want to be studying psychology at university. I want to be moved out. I want to have my life in order.

Millie at
Edinburgh Gardens.

Meet the Photographer

EREMAYA ALBRECHT

20
Alice Springs,
AUSTRALIA

When Eremaya's not taking photos:
"I work and I study. I love art, reading, hanging out with my friends, adventuring, and being outside."

Something most people don't know about her:
"I am an aerialist."

> "There are two beds in my room. I mostly use the left one. It's more comfortable."
>
> —Mahak, INDIA

A Room of One's Own

Jung Eun, of South Korea, texting from bed.

Anyone who remembers being a teen knows: Bedrooms are our sanctuary. These 18-year-olds agree.

Shenzi, of China, in her favorite spot.

"My room is my sanctuary. My private space."

—Hélène,
LOS ANGELES

—Millie,
AUSTRALIA

"My room is my temple. I brought my tapestries and lights from home to give my dorm the same feel."

—Grace, WASHINGTON, D.C.

Anndrine at home in Norway.

Mahak Naiwal
New Delhi, India

Mahak is studying in school and learning kathak, a traditional Indian dance.

PHOTOGRAPHED BY Shraddha Gupta

"Everybody says that after 18 years, life changes. I am very excited and would like to celebrate my 18th birthday in a grand way—with my family and friends, by going out for dinner."

Mahak performing puja, a type of prayer, at home.

21

Mahak rehearsing in her
kathak class.

Mahak at a
house party with
friends.

If you could have dinner with anyone, dead or alive, who would it be?
My grandfather. He was very close to me. I often remember him very fondly. He was a good person, nature-wise. He suffered from some mental troubles. I was very little when he was around.

What would you like to ask him?
First, I would like to offer him his favorite food. I would like to prepare tea for him. I would cook daal-chawal (lentils and rice) and also roti (hand-rolled bread). And then I would talk to him for a long time. I would share with him my life's experiences in the past years. I would also share some memories of my childhood. When I was a small child, he used to feed me. Sometimes he would pretend he was a horse. I enjoyed it very much, I remember. His behavior was very childish.

Where do you see yourself in the future?

I would like to develop myself into a teacher. I am very keen to study political science. Also, I will continue learning dancing.

What are you looking forward to about being an adult?

I am excited about casting a vote. Casting a vote means being a responsible citizen. Apart from being excited, I also have some tension as I am turning 18. I think a lot about my future. I spend a good amount of time planning my future studies. I am also trying to be as independent as possible to make my life stable in the future.

Meet the Photographer

SHRADDHA GUPTA

19
Palampur,
Himachal Pradesh,
INDIA

When Shraddha's not taking photos:
"I read or watch movies and I like spending time walking around in the city. Sometimes I go cycling too."

Something most people don't know about her:
"I am really shy."

What's Your Family Tradition?

"Every two weeks my family eats hot pot together, and every week we eat fish. This is because my family likes to eat hot pot, so when we're eating hot pot, everyone is happy, and it makes it easy to communicate with each other."

—Shenzi, CHINA

"Sometimes, rarely, we have big family board game nights, but they end up getting so competitive and everyone ends up hating each other at the end."

—Millie, AUSTRALIA

"After every three months we must meet as a family. Whenever we meet there must be lots of food."

—Wanjiku, KENYA

"On Día de la Virgen we have a shrine and we celebrate the Virgin. Sometimes we will kill a hen to pretend like we're giving the Virgin something to eat."

—Obdulia, MEXICO

"We offer puja together. We distribute sweets during Diwali. Relatives visit us. During Janmashtami (an annual festival to celebrate the birth of the Hindu god Krishna), we decorate the room of Lord Krishna in our house with many balloons. We fast during this celebration. We stay up until midnight and cut cakes."

—Mahak, INDIA

"Every year we go out to a different state for a couple of days. This year we're trying to go to New Jersey. Last year we went to Delaware. The year before we went to Dorney Park, an amusement park in Pennsylvania. Hopefully next year we try to go somewhere farther."

—Maryclare, THE BRONX

Hélène Françoise Philippe
Los Angeles, California

Hélène is a student at CalArts, where she studies fine art and animation. Her mother emigrated from Guadalajara, Mexico, and her dad from Nassau, Bahamas.

PHOTOGRAPHED BY Arleigh Haskal

Who do you go to for advice?
My mom. I don't have any siblings. She's the only one who raised me. So definitely my mom. She's like my rock. Recently, I watched *Gilmore Girls* and I felt like it was talking about my life. That strong mother-daughter bond is exactly what I have.

Do you miss your family now that you're away at college?
Yes and no. I did live with my family my entire life, basically like a Mexican *Full House*. So it is hard to part from them. But I think, as somebody who is the first in my family to go to college, it's very big for them. So I just want to focus on what I have to focus on here, and then have my weekends with my family. But I definitely miss them.

Hélène and a friend on the fire escape of her home.

Where's your favorite place to be inside your home?
Oh, definitely my room.

What about outside?
I love Chinatown so much. And I love going to boba shops.

What's a place you've never been but would most like to go?
I'm a huge Dolly Parton fan. She's like one of my big inspirations. Her fashion, the way she presents herself, she's just very her own, and I really love that. So I'd like to go to Dollywood, her theme park, in Tennessee.

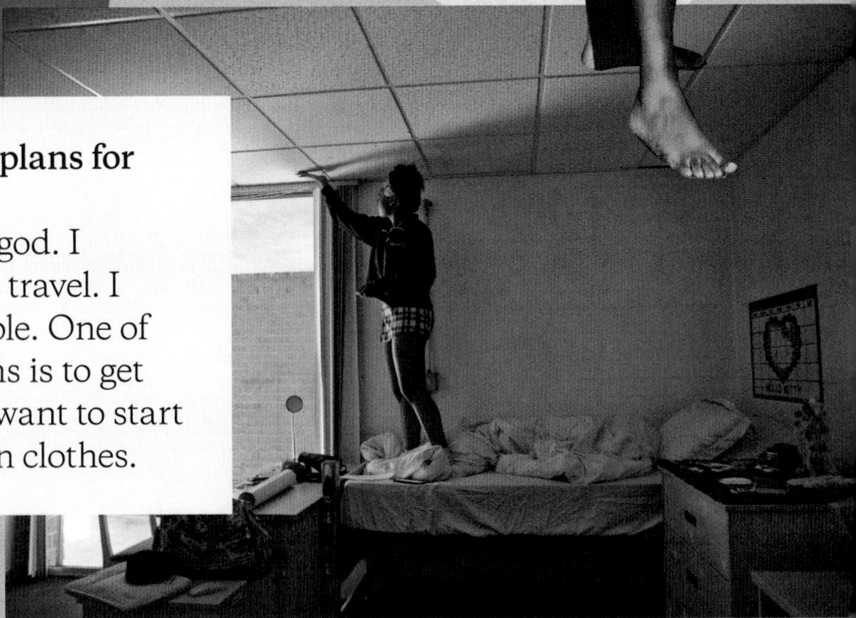

Clockwise from left:
Hélène admiring her
first-ever art print; at
the beach with friends;
decorating her dorm room.

Do you have any plans for the future?

So many. Oh my god. I definitely want to travel. I want to help people. One of my biggest dreams is to get my PhD in art. I want to start designing my own clothes.

What about fears?
It might be a tad weird, but I always tell myself that the worst possible scenario that could ever happen in any situation is that you wind up dead. So like, if somebody punches you in the face, you can recover from that. If something embarrassing happens, you can recover from that. So as long as I'm not dying, like—I'll be okay.

What are you looking forward to about being 18?
Eighteen is that little gray spot between adulthood and childhood. You're still a little kid, but the world is like, "You're a grown-up," and you somehow have to merge the two.

Hélène and friends
hang out.

Meet the Photographer

ARLEIGH HASKAL

17
Los Angeles,
CALIFORNIA

When Arleigh's not taking photos: She's a high school student who enjoys being with her friends, swimming, and playing the guitar. She helps coach a swim team for elementary school students.

Something most people don't know about her: "When I was little, a ladybug used to fly to my window every day. I knew it was the same one because it only had one spot. I named her 'Sandy' after my preschool teacher."

Liana Sharifian
Bushehr, Iran

Liana is among the few Iranian women who play the bagpipe. She recently performed in an all-women show in Tehran.

PHOTOGRAPHED BY Atefe Moeini

What's a place you've never been but would like to visit?

Many places. Like the U.S.—I really want to go there! And England because of the bagpipes. I really want to go listen to Scottish bagpipes. I love beach countries too, like the Maldives for relaxed vacations. I'd also love to go to Egypt, but we Iranians can't go. I usually love to go to places that you can't go.

Liana playing the bagpipe; below, with her best friend at a beach where only men are allowed to swim.

What is something you'd like to learn to do?
Singing.

You like to sing?
A lot! I really want women singing to be allowed in our country. They sing so beautifully. We have so many good voices. I'd also like to learn to swim.

What is your favorite part about performing with other women?
I can be my real self. I can play from the bottom of my heart, whereas in men's concerts you have to be really careful your scarf doesn't fall off or something like that.

Liana on the right, talking to friends before a concert in Tehran.

What's the mood like in these women-only concerts?

It is good. It makes me happy that we have these freedoms. But you know what's bad and painful? That we are not able to film or take photos at the shows. I have friends in Spain and other countries who ask, "What are you doing today?" And when I am like, "I have a concert," they say, "Oh, send us a video!" Then I have to explain to them that this is a women-only concert and you are not able to film or take photos. It is hard for them to believe! But at least it is good that our fellow women can hear us play. I am happy when I see they can clap and move around.

What was the last music you listened to?
I listen to music each and every second.
I listen to everything—sonati (traditional
Persian music), foreign music, young
people music, rap music. All of it together.
I want to listen to everything to see what
people like.

Where do you see yourself in 5 years?
I'd really like to know a lot about the
bagpipe and I'd like to be one of the best.
Right now, all I think of is the bagpipe.

Liana with
her grandfather.

"I have 20,000 selfies.
I love taking pictures."

Meet the Photographer

ATEFE MOEINI

20
Bushehr,
IRAN

When Atefe's not taking photos:
"I'm interested to know more about my society and the world we live in today. Literature and news help me a lot in this way—so when I don't take pictures, I spend most of my time reading books and following the news."

Something most people don't know about her:
"I used to play football with boys in my elementary school, and I was a goalkeeper. In Iran, boys and girls have separate schools, but in our school we both studied together, which was rare. In that time my father used to teach me some skills about football every day."

The last song these girls
listened to was . . .

#This Is 18

A Mixtape

GRRRL PWR!

A

Kweku – CHIEF OBI

Wo!! – OLAMIDE

God Is a Woman – ARIANA GRANDE

ABCs of New York – PRINCESS NOKIA

No Me Pidas Perdón – BANDA SINALOENSE MS DE SERGIO LIZÁRRAGA

Billie Jean – MICHAEL JACKSON

Ashegh Shodan – MOHSEN EBRAHIMZADEH

Zahav – STATIC & BEN EL

Shape of You – ED SHEERAN

Audio – LSD (SIA, DIPLO, AND LABRINTH)

Ay Vatan – AHDEYEH

Home with You – MADISON BEER

B

Nwa Baby – DAVIDO

Mr. Blue Sky – ELECTRIC LIGHT ORCHESTRA

Run – SYNCYB, DAM, AND LUKITASCMK

Born to Live – SERGEY MAVRIN

Futile Devices – SUFJAN STEVENS

Angel Eyes – THE CAST OF *MAMMA MIA! HERE WE GO AGAIN*

Skyline To – FRANK OCEAN

Intense 2018 – ANDRÉ NILSEN

Strawberry Fields Forever – THE BEATLES

Spis din Syvende Sans – KARPE DIEM

Life on Mars? – DAVID BOWIE

She Remembers Everything – ROSANNE CASH FEATURING SAM PHILLIPS

Obdulia González González
Zacatecas, Mexico

Obdulia is part of the indigenous Wixárika people of northern Mexico. She helps her parents sell traditional crafts and hopes to attend college.

PHOTOGRAPHED BY Jesse Mireles

When did you first feel like a grown-up?
When I was 15, my mother let me go to my hometown of San Sebastián by myself for the first time. I attended the patron saints' festivals. I had to fight for her to let me go because she said I was too young. I was there for the entire duration of the party, which was like 3 or 4 days. At the end, I thought, "I am an adult; I'm allowed to travel by myself."

After that, did your mother allow you to do more things?
Yes—for instance, yesterday, I went to the movies with my friends.

Obdulia with her mother, Alicia.

49

Obdulia with her younger sister Alondra.

"I'm proud of my culture and my heritage. I love dressing in a different way and speaking a different, beautiful language. For example, in Wixárika, 'tsineka areuyajuwa' means 'I love you.'"

Tell us about a family tradition.

On Día de la Virgen we have a shrine and we celebrate the Virgin. Sometimes we will kill a hen to pretend like we're giving the Virgin something to eat. And we do the same on New Year's. At midnight, we also kill a hen, and we ask God for the coming year to be good for us. We also place money, the first money we made the day before, to have a better year.

Obdulia and her mother sing the Mexican national anthem.

Obdulia with handmade
bracelets and making an
embroidered pouch.

What do you do when you are bored?
I listen to music, watch movies, go downtown, meet my cousin.

What's something you'd like to learn how to do?
To be able to use a computer better, dance bachata, and drive.

What do you hope to be doing in 5 years?
I hope to finish high school and be studying in college and to work in something other than making crafts all the time.

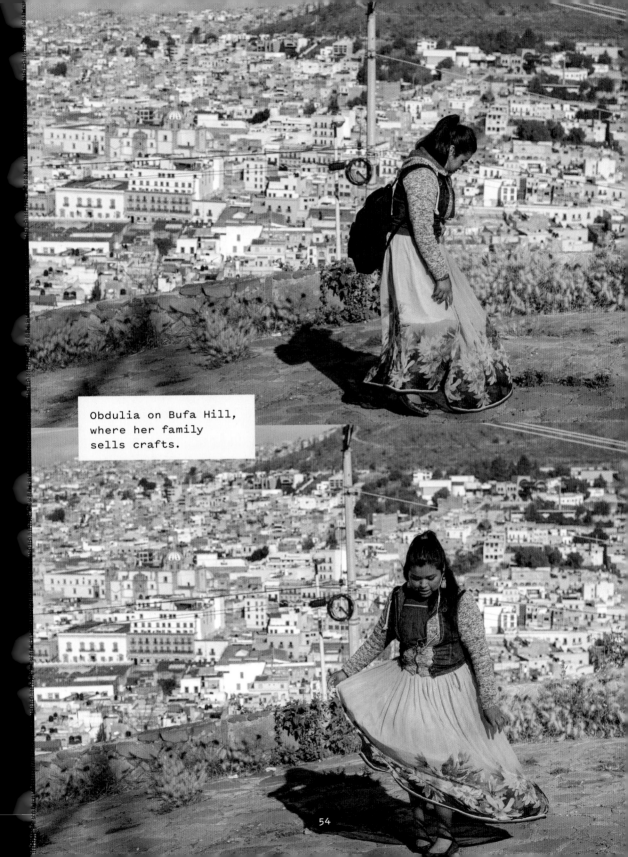

Obdulia on Bufa Hill, where her family sells crafts.

Meet the Photographer

JESSE MIRELES

20
Zacatecas,
MEXICO

When Jesse's not taking photos:
"I'm reading my favorite books or learning how to dance on my own. Or perhaps hiking with my friends or in an antique store looking for some old cameras. But even then, my camera is always with me."

Something most people don't know about her:
"When I was 12 years old, my dream was to star in a musical on Broadway. I spent time in my room dancing and performing with the music of *Cats*, imagining that hundreds of people came to Broadway just to see me!"

Maryclare Chinedo
The Bronx, New York

Maryclare is studying biochemistry at Brown University.

PHOTOGRAPHED BY Julie Lozano

What is the farthest you've been from home?
In 2013, my sister and I went to school in Nigeria for two years, where my parents are from. It was hard, but I'm grateful for how much I learned. It taught me to do as much as I could with little resources, which has made me appreciate what's given to me here in the States. I also learned to appreciate my culture more.

Maryclare at her local train station.

Who do you go to for advice?
I go to my friends because I know they won't judge me.

What do you do when you're bored?
Netflix, Netflix, Netflix. Right now, I'm watching *The Vampire Diaries*. I just finished *The Office*.

What's one thing you'd like to learn?
I don't know how to cook. When I was younger, I was taught that I have to know how to cook for my husband and children, and I don't really like that. So I just didn't want to learn how to cook at all. But now I think knowing how to cook is a good thing to have—not for a man or my kids but for myself.

Maryclare takes a selfie on Snapchat; below, with a writing mentor.

Maryclare with parents Don and Stella and siblings Emma, Don, and Chelsea; below, with Chelsea, 13.

Prior to college, Maryclare
volunteered at a nursing
home and worked at
McDonald's (above).

When did you first feel like an adult?
I think I first felt like a grown-up when my mom let me go to the after-prom party. My mom doesn't usually let me go out. I would never be able to go to the parties my friends invited me to in high school, but she let me go to this one. I talked to her in private and told her that in America it's a tradition to go to your after-prom party. She was a bit mad, but she let me go. I guess it's because she knows that I'm 18 and I'll be going to college soon. After-prom was weird since I've never really been to a party before, but I had fun.

Selfies with best
friend Jessy, center,
and sister Chelsea.

Meet the Photographer

JULIE LOZANO

18
South Bronx,
NEW YORK

Something most people don't know about her:
"I like to put lime and Tajín on my Lay's."

When Julie's not taking photos:
"You'll probably find me at my film school or skateboarding with my friends."

Shama Ghosh
Chandpur, Bangladesh

Shama lives with her husband and his family in a Hindu neighborhood in Chandpur. She hopes to finish high school and become a teacher.

PHOTOGRAPHED BY Tahia Farhin Haque

Is there any particular tradition in your family—something you do every year, every week, or daily?
I perform puja once in the morning and once at night.

Who do you go to for advice?
If I make a mistake, I will turn to the elders in the family like my father-in-law and mother-in-law. In more serious situations, I will seek advice from my mother.

What do you do in your spare time?
Sometimes I watch television. When my aunts visit our place, I chat with them. I spend my time this way.

What are your favorite spots in and outside your home?

I don't really travel much; I just go to school and return here. But there is one place I love—I love visiting my grandmother, staying with her. I enjoy eating the food she makes.

What is something you would like to do or learn?

Getting an education, followed by a job. As a child, I wanted to be a policeman. Now, my husband says that it would be nice if I study well and become a teacher.

Shama babysitting her sister-in-law's twins.

Shama getting ready in the mirror; below, performing puja, a type of prayer, with her mother-in-law.

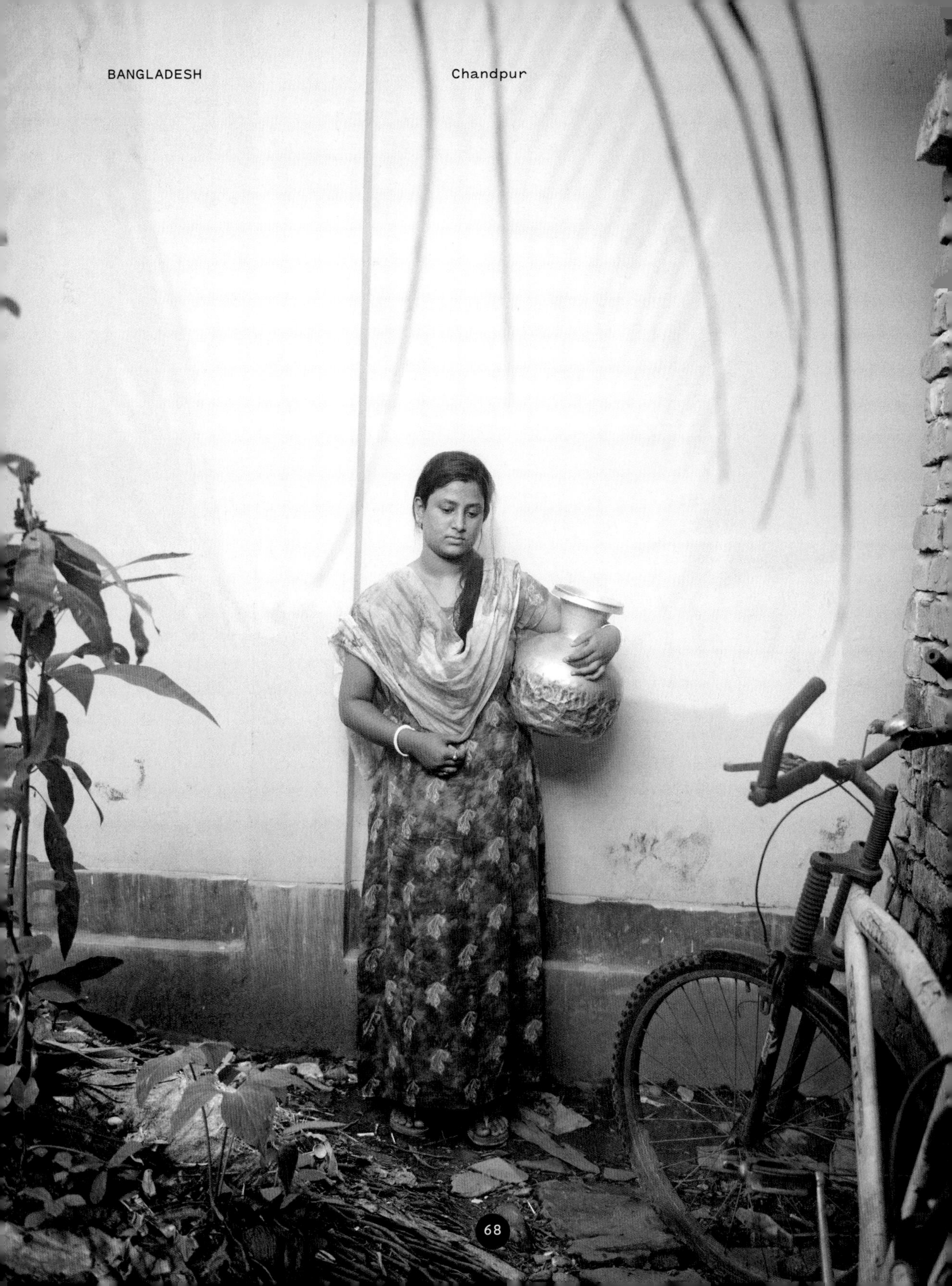

What do you hope for your future?
I am completely concentrated on
my family, of course. Once a girl is
married, she cannot do anything
without the permission of her
family. If there is anything I want to
do now, I have to ask my husband
and other family members first.
If I can ever manage to stand on
my own feet and do something on
my own, then my future would be
really bright.

Shama in her
school uniform.

Meet the Photographer

TAHIA FARHIN HAQUE

22
Dhaka,
BANGLADESH

Something most people don't know about her: "I buy books in abundance."

When Tahia's not taking photos: "I'm studying biochemistry at North South University or roaming around my city, Dhaka, looking for new places."

How I Get

"I just got a bike, but I'm still in the process of putting it together."

–Grace, WASHINGTON, D.C.

"When I go to dance practice, I usually just walk, and if I'm going to work, I usually take the 2 train."

–Maryclare, THE BRONX

"Sometimes the bus, or a taxi, and I walk too."

–Obdulia, MEXICO

"I usually get around by gua gua (public bus), and in taxis only when I am in a hurry. I'm not a big fan of the gua guas though. They are very crowded, very hot and crammed."

–Thalia, CUBA

Around

"I now have a driver's license, so I drive around a lot. Very little bus, a lot of car."

—Anndrine, NORWAY

"Taxi."

—Liana, IRAN

"I travel back and forth by auto rickshaw."

—Shama, BANGLADESH

"I usually take a minibus or walk."

—Faiza, WEST BANK

"I travel by scooty."

—Mahak, INDIA

Victory Chukwu
Lagos, Nigeria

Victory is a student at the University of Lagos. She lives with her mother.

PHOTOGRAPHED BY Amarachi Chukwuma
AND Ebunoluwa Osaro Akinbo

What's the farthest you've been from home?
The headquarters of our church in Ibadan, Oyo State. It takes all day to get there from Yaba, Lagos, where I live.

Where would you like to visit?
My dream place to visit is Paris. I just want to experience the Eiffel Tower. I want to take pictures there, visit, eat the food.

If you could have dinner with anyone, dead or alive, who would it be?
For people alive, I would love to have dinner with Migos. But for the dead, it would have to be Whitney Houston.

What do you do when you feel bored?
My music keeps me company. Mostly slow Christian music like Don Moen while I'm bored and trap music when I'm trying to be hype.

What's one thing you don't know how to do that you'd like to learn?
I'd like to learn how to cook some Nigerian soups. I don't eat traditional food, but I want to learn to cook in case I marry one day.

Victory helps a market vendor pack yams into her shopping bag.

Victory and her mother prepare
a meal in their kitchen.

When did you first feel like a grown-up?
I first felt like an adult when I went to the market without my mum and got everything she wanted. It made me feel grown to bargain with the sellers and get the best prices.

What do you want to be doing in 5 years?
Five years from now I'll have finished school and intend to be working as a self-made woman. I want to be a fashion designer.

Victory, in
yellow, at church
with her mother.

Victory, right, with her mom and a friend, notice baby crabs in the water by her home.

What are you most looking forward to about being 18?
I want to drive.

Do you have a life motto?
Good food and lit friends: That's my recipe for a healthy life.

Meet the Photographer

AMARACHI CHUKWUMA

19
Lagos,
NIGERIA
and
NEW JERSEY

Something most people don't know about her: "I'm a secret country music fan."

When Amarachi's not taking photos: She's a college student in New Jersey.

Meet the Photographer

EBUNOLUWA OSARO AKINBO

24
Lagos,
NIGERIA

When Ebunoluwa's not taking photos:
"I'm either researching photography projects, reading photography books, or hanging out with friends."

Something most people don't know about her:
"I run a food business called Bunbun Foods. I prepare finger foods and snacks and mail meals like jollof rice."

Anndrine Lund
Rena, Norway

Anndrine attends high school in the town of Hamar and plans to study political science. She works part-time at IKEA.

PHOTOGRAPHED BY Celina Christoffersen

What do you eat for breakfast?
When I eat breakfast on weekdays, it's quick, maybe fruit or something. During the weekends with the family, we have breakfast together with bread rolls and coffee where Mom puts up a nice setup. It's my favorite meal, breakfast during the weekends. Dad works a lot. He is an ambulance driver and can work 24/7, so he is not always with us at breakfast. But when the three of us are home—or even two of us—we always eat breakfast and dinner together. It's very cozy.

Anndrine at home with her mom and brother.

If you could have dinner with anyone, who would it be?
There is always a better answer to this question, because there are so many cool people. But sometimes I think Trump, or even Sylvi Listhaug (Norway's minister of immigration), because we have such different opinions. To just be able to sit and have dinner with them and say whatever damn thing I feel like—that would be so cool.

What do you do when you feel bored?
When I feel bored, I watch movies, try to do things with my friends, or just chill on the couch with my phone.

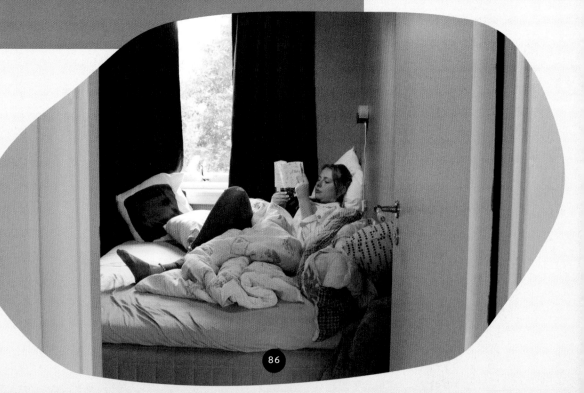

Anndrine and her mother in the kitchen.

What's your favorite place inside your home?

Where I live now, it must be the couch. Where I used to live, it was my bedroom, because the bedroom was the most private place. Now I have an apartment for myself, and I feel more comfortable on the couch. It's cozier there than in my room.

What about outside your home?
In my car maybe, not because it's fun to drive around but because I listen to loud music and sing and just think all different thoughts and just be myself 110 percent. I don't know, I just feel like myself when I am driving, because I am usually alone.

What's something you'd like to learn?
I don't know if I can learn it, but I would love to learn how to sing.

Childhood photos
of Anndrine.

Anndrine eating lunch
with friends (above);
making a poster as
part of a political
youth group she's
involved in.

Meet the Photographer

CELINA CHRISTOFFERSEN

22
Hamar,
NORWAY

When Celina's not taking photos:
"I like spending my time with family and friends, doing something fun or just talking. I also spend a lot of time engaging in local and national politics."

Something most people don't know about her:
"When I was younger, I participated in *Norway's Got Talent*—twice. It turned out my talent was NOT singing."

Table for 12?

Chimamanda
Ngozi
Adichie

Anne of
Green
Gables

David
Bowie

Migos

Donald
Trump

From Socrates to Whitney Houston, here's who the girls would like to invite to their dinner party.

Timothée Chalamet

Princess Nokia

Mikhail Yuryevich Lermontov

Whitney Houston

Socrates

Thalia Curbelo Márquez
Havana, Cuba

Thalia lives with her aunt and cousins and is studying industrial engineering. She likes exercising, American television, and music.

PHOTOGRAPHED BY Alexandra Álvarez

What kind of music do you like?
I like listening to music with headphones.
I prefer music in English when I want to
relax, but I can listen to anything, really. I
don't like to listen to reggaetón unless I'm
at a party. I know the songs, I've learned
the lyrics, but I'm not a big fan.

Is there anything you'd like to learn but haven't had the chance?
How to cook well. I can cook basic stuff, but I'm not a great cook.

What would you like to cook?
Desserts. I love desserts. Something simple and yummy. I know how to make torrejas, arepas, but I'd like to learn to bake and make a cake.

Thalia with her cousins.

Is cooking a big part of your family traditions?
Some of my family traditions are with my aunt
and my cousins, like celebrating New Year's
and Mother's Day, when the whole family
gets together at my grandmother's house. We
have lunch together, and everybody prepares
something. We always have pork—it's so tasty—
and beans, that's a regular . . . rice, fried banana,
potatoes, bread, a salad. We have soft drinks,
and sometimes beer, because my aunt likes it
very much. For dessert, we have pudding or
crème caramel. Sometimes I make torrejas,
because that's my thing.

Who do you go to for advice?
My aunt. She is the youngest, and I've always talked to her honestly. I can speak to her about things that I can't discuss with anyone else. She really understands me and always tries to help me.

Do you feel any different now that you are 18?
I feel the same. It's just one more year. They say that from now on time moves faster, but I feel the same.

Thalia at home
with family.

Meet the Photographer

ALEXANDRA ÁLVAREZ

19
Havana,
CUBA

What Alexandra does when she's not taking photos:
She attends school and loves reading comics.

Something most people don't know about her:
"I like to write poems and stories in my free time."

Madison Breanne Justice
Clarksdale, Mississippi

Madison is taking a break from school to work and support her son, Jeremiah. She hopes to complete her GED and attend college.

PHOTOGRAPHED BY Yasmine Malone

What's a superpower you wish you had?
I wish I could read people's minds so I could know what they're thinking.

Madison with her friend Staci; below, eating dinner with Staci, Jeremiah, and friends.

How do you think being a young mother has changed your path?

I had to think about my future a lot faster. My goal before was that I wanted to go and finish high school. I wanted to graduate and go to college and get away from here. And now since I've had a kid, I had to drop out of school because I didn't have no one to babysit, really, or help me watch him much. And then since I couldn't go to school, I had to get a job. Now my goal is getting a better job, getting my GED, and trying to get out of here as fast as possible.

What would you like to study?

Well, I really wanted to be an art major because I have a passion for art. Ever since I saw my dad sketching and my big sister drawing cartoon animals, it was like, "I want to do that. That looks so cool." Now I see people getting tattoos and that looks amazing. I want to be a tattoo artist now.

Do you like to draw anything in particular?
When I first started drawing, I drew everything and anything—from vases to flowers to the trees. Nature I guess is pretty cool to me. When I was pregnant, I had this baby book and I would draw a picture on every page. I would draw little animals and stuff . . . that was cool for me.

What do you do when you feel bored?
When I get bored and Jeremiah's awake, I go outside and let him play in the pool. When I'm bored and he's asleep, I love to sketch. Or sometimes just lay there.

"I try to make Jeremiah and me go to the park at least once a week just to get outside and have him play. I love seeing him at the park. He loves the swing."

When did you first feel like a grown-up?
I first felt like a grown-up when I was pretty much halfway into my pregnancy, because I realized that everything was about to change.

What the farthest place you've been from home?
The farthest I've ever been away from my house is three hours away, in Dyersburg, like right there on the edge of Missouri. My grandmother lives there. I really wish I'd been farther because I would love to see new things. I would love to see a waterfall in my life.

Madison with friends after her shift. She works at a coffee shop. At right, with her brother.

Madison outside her parents' home. She does not live with them, and yearns for a bigger space of her own.

Meet the Photographer

YASMINE MALONE

20
Clarksdale,
MISSISSIPPI

When Yasmine's not taking photos:
She is pursuing a dual degree in political science and English at the University of Mississippi.

Something most people don't know about her:
"I have a fraternal twin sister."

I'm Bored. What Should I Do?

START HERE

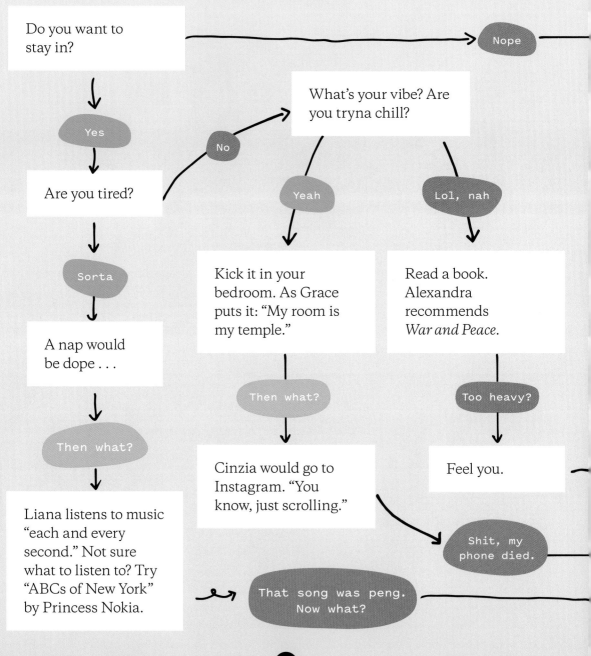

Do you want to stay in?

Nope

Yes

Are you tired?

No

What's your vibe? Are you tryna chill?

Sorta

Yeah

Lol, nah

A nap would be dope . . .

Kick it in your bedroom. As Grace puts it: "My room is my temple."

Read a book. Alexandra recommends *War and Peace.*

Then what?

Then what?

Too heavy?

Liana listens to music "each and every second." Not sure what to listen to? Try "ABCs of New York" by Princess Nokia.

Cinzia would go to Instagram. "You know, just scrolling."

Feel you.

Shit, my phone died.

That song was peng. Now what?

Spoiler: It's probably Netflix.

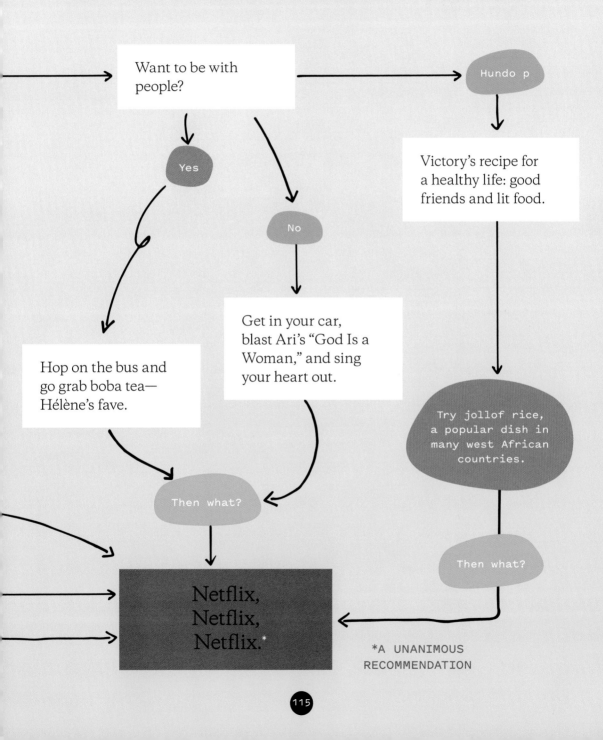

Want to be with people?

Hundo p

Yes

No

Victory's recipe for a healthy life: good friends and lit food.

Hop on the bus and go grab boba tea—Hélène's fave.

Get in your car, blast Ari's "God Is a Woman," and sing your heart out.

Try jollof rice, a popular dish in many west African countries.

Then what?

Then what?

Netflix, Netflix, Netflix.*

*A UNANIMOUS RECOMMENDATION

Faiza Al-Afifi
Ramallah, West Bank

Faiza is studying international law at a university in Rabat, Morocco. Her family has been in Ramallah since 2014, when they fled the Gaza Strip after its war with Israel.

PHOTOGRAPHED BY Leen Awartani

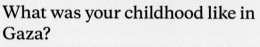

24. Don't give up just because of what someone said. Use that as a motivation to push HARDER.

What was your childhood like in Gaza?

Gaza used to be beautiful. I used to skateboard in the street and ride my bicycle.

Did growing up during a war affect your outlook?

My childhood in Gaza has certainly affected my personality. I matured faster because of the harsh conditions there, not to mention that Gaza is like a prison—you cannot move or go places freely. We were surrounded from all directions. The Israeli occupation affects the lives of all the people living there, whether they are young or old.

Faiza loves
reading. She says
it gives her a
sense of serenity.

Faiza with her
best friend Zeina.

Tell me about your job.
I work at an aquarium. I actually operate the photo booth—taking photos and putting backgrounds behind them, like fishes and things. It's really awesome. I could have gone and worked at a café, but I really wanted to do something that had meaning, where I could learn something new. I've learned a lot about fishes, their names and where they come from, what kind of water they live in, the weather they live in. It's really interesting.

Faiza and Zeina
spend time outside.

What do you hope to be doing in 5 years?
I want to be in a place where I feel happy, to be a productive and effective person in society and life. I survived more than three wars. My goal in life now is to be a contributor—to defend basic human rights and to help people in need. This is what I'd like to achieve.

121

Faiza and her
brothers at home.

Meet the Photographer

LEEN AWARTANI

19
Ramallah,
WEST BANK

When Leen's not taking photos:
She is studying law at Maastricht University in the Netherlands. She writes poetry for fun.

Something most people don't know about her:
"I base my outfit choices on historic fashion movements."

Alexandra Yuryeva
Moscow, Russia

Alexandra lives at home with her parents and younger sister. She enjoys synchronized swimming, art, and physics.

PHOTOGRAPHED BY Anna Dermicheva

What was the last song you listened to?
It was a song by Sergey Mavrin called "Born to Live." It is a rock song—relatively heavy but inspiring music that motivates you not to waste time, not to regret anything, not to blame anyone but yourself for the problems you have and to somehow deal with it.

If you could have dinner with anyone, who would it be?

For the living, it would be my closest female friend. For the dead, it would be Mikhail Yuryevich Lermontov, the Russian romance poet. I'd listen to him. Or maybe it would be my father. He'd inspire me. He left when I was one, and I know virtually nothing about him—well, besides what my mother told me, that he was ambitious and aimed high. But as they say, he who chases two rabbits will catch neither.

Alexandra recently began playing the balalaika, a traditional Russian string instrument.

What's your favorite place in your house?
Perhaps it is my balcony—I used to sleep in it. Of course, no sea or mountains were visible, just a regular cityscape, but it was still beautiful in the morning.

What about outside your home?
There is a village not far from my neighborhood, and between the village and my home there is a road that stretches for about three kilometers. Along that road there are fields, and pines grow there. That's the place where I really like to go for walks. The sky is very beautiful there. When I have nothing else to do in the summer, I explore the area, get on a bicycle and ride to parts unknown.

What do you want to be doing in 5 years?

Maybe, after graduating from God-knows-what university, I'd engage in theoretical physics or go for nuclear power engineering. I'd like to develop nuclear plant security systems so Chernobyl doesn't happen again.

In the park with her friend Elena.

What are you looking forward to about being 18?

I'm waiting for the time when I can swing on a swing in the courtyard at midnight, and when law enforcement officers come up to me, I'll just show them my ID and they will leave. (Russia has a curfew for minors.) I don't know if that's strange or not, but in my mind 18 is associated with swinging on a swing for hours and listening to cool music while others smoke and drink. So I'm waiting for the moment when I'll be able to do this legally.

As the eldest child, Alexandra's household chores include making breakfast and taking her sister Varvara to school.

Sharing a laugh with Elena and Varvara.

Meet the Photographer

ANNA DERMICHEVA

20
Moscow,
RUSSIA

When Anna's not taking photos:
She is a university student studying sociology and loves reading and travel.

Something most people don't know about her:
"I am in love with horses and equestrian sports!" She is saving money to buy herself a horse.

"How we value each other as human beings living on this planet."
−Grace, WASHINGTON, D.C.

"Who am I going to be? Am I going to be known? I'm worried that I'm not going to be known, and if I die no one would know who I am."
−Victory, NIGERIA

Here's What

"Global warming. Some people think global warming is a hoax. They think that dropping trash on the floor once is not contributing to global warming when it is."
−Maryclare, THE BRONX

"People are becoming more anti-immigrant and welfare benefits are falling—the ones who get the most are getting even more. People who don't have that much get less."
−Anndrine, NORWAY

"More than anything else, being a girl. There is no safety here in Delhi."
—Mahak, INDIA

"Forgetting the local music. I love ancient Iran, and forgetting customs and practices makes me feel concerned. It is very beautiful to save our local customs."
—Liana, IRAN

Worries Me

"I'm afraid that the new generation will forget about things like also going outside or reading a book because everything is just phone, phone, phone."
—Cinzia, GERMANY

"Environmental protection. All the garbage that's thrown into the sea, many animals are becoming extinct—this is very worrisome."
—Lior, ISRAEL

Ruby Jubb-Baddiel
London, U.K.

Ruby has a year left of high school and hopes to attend college after.

PHOTOGRAPHED BY Georgia Canning

Looking at the world today, what worries you about the future?
The environment.

Really?
Yeah. We're gonna ruin the world. That's quite scary. And I feel like social media has corrupted our generation a bit. We are meant to be this generation of new hope, but it's all so warped.

Ruby, center, with friends Mia and Megan after school.

With friends Mia and
Megan preparing to
take a swim.

What's one thing you don't know how to do that you'd like to learn?
I would say sing, but I feel like you don't *not* know how to sing. Maybe to cook a bit better. I can still pick up a recipe and figure it out, but to be able to actually cook.

When did you first feel like a grown-up?
I remember being able to walk to school on my own, and I thought, "Wow! I am so independent and cool."

What do you want to be doing in 5 years?
I don't know. I want to say the right thing.
I'd like to have not a set career but to be
doing something I like that I know can
go somewhere. Not just end up finishing
university and be working as a waitress
not really knowing what to do.

Tell us about a family tradition.
It's not really a tradition, but my
dad and his family have made-up
words. I genuinely, until I was like 11,
thought they were real words. Such as
"glemsonning," which means staring into
the distance. I thought it was a real word.

Ruby taking a break from
rhythmic gymnastics.

Ruby, center,
chilling with
friends.

Meet the Photographer

GEORGIA CANNING

20
Surrey,
ENGLAND

When Georgia's not taking photos:
She's a fashion assistant at a magazine and works in a pub on the weekends.

Something most people don't know about her:
She's a film nut. "I once watched a film every day for six months. Another time a friend and I spent 12 hours in a cinema."

Sage Grace
Dolan-Sandrino
Washington, D.C.

Grace is a transgender student
who attends Bard College in New
York. She is a student activist and
aspiring filmmaker.

PHOTOGRAPHED BY TiKa Wallace

What place have you never been that you would like to go?
My dad actually asks me this all the time. One place that I've never been that I would really like to go to is the coast of France or Italy or Spain. And I've been to Cuba, but it was when I was very young, and I'd really like to go back.

Is your family Cuban?
Yeah. My dad's side is Cuban.

Who do you go to for advice?
I go to my family, and my family is not just my parents but a group of friends who have become my family. They're the people who know the most about me, how I act, why I act, what affects my actions, and they're the people I can go to for counsel and advice.

Do you have a favorite place inside your home?
I love my room; my room is my temple. I brought my tapestries and lights from home to give my dorm the same feel. It's important that I feel comfortable in my room and am able to decompress.

What do you see yourself doing in 5 years?
Producing, directing, creating. I want to have a production company that is dedicated to giving young artists a platform to tell their stories.

Such as?
The stories of young trans girls at college. These are stories that may be told by mainstream Hollywood, but not by the people who have lived them.

Do you like being alone?
There is something about learning how to be alone that for me has come both by choice and by necessity. Being alone for me is not always being lonely.

When did you first feel like a grown-up?
I really felt responsible my first night at college, with all the choices that were in front of me. Do I go out? Do I stay in? Do I eat ramen? Do I eat healthy? Do I stay up? Do I go to bed? Those are questions that I face every day, along with many more. But I think the presentation of these choices—choices that are for me and only me to make—have definitely made me feel like a grown-up.

Grace eats lunch with
a friend; above, at the
school library.

Grace in her dorm room.

Meet the Photographer

TIKA WALLACE

18
Falls Church,
VIRGINIA

Something most people don't know about her:
"I know three languages: English, 'cause America, French because of school, and American Sign Language because I said I was bored one day, and my mother told me to go learn ASL."

When TiKa's not taking photos:
"I am usually reading or doing homework. Or procrastinating about doing homework."

Jung Eun Yang
Sokcho, South Korea

Jung Eun is preparing for her college entrance exam. Her dream is to become a makeup artist.

PHOTOGRAPHED BY Da Hyeon Kim

What's your favorite place inside your home?
My room.

And outside your home?
The stairs behind my friend's house, where we can sit together.

What do you do when you feel bored?
I often ask a friend to come out and we sit outside and talk.

Texting with friends.

Jung Eun practices
body painting on a
mannequin, above, and
at right, a model.

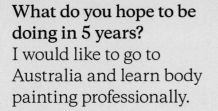

What do you hope to be doing in 5 years?
I would like to go to Australia and learn body painting professionally.

What worries you about the future?
I am most concerned about global warming. I am scared that summer will become hotter.

At a beach near
her home.

When did you first feel like an adult?
When I was young, I easily grew tired of whatever I was doing and quickly gave up on it, even if it was something I liked to do. But since I started learning makeup skills, I have persistently kept at it. Even when I went to school after staying up all night finishing a project, I felt a rush of happiness and pride rather than thinking it felt hard to wake up and go to school. And when I realized how rewarding this was, I felt that I grew up a lot and became a bit of an adult.

What are you looking forward to about being 18? In Korea, becoming 18 means that you have reached an age when you are finalizing your days at school before going out into the real world. To me, it represents the year I made the most effort to live to my fullest before becoming an adult.

Meet the Photographer

DA HYEON KIM

18
Cheongju,
SOUTH KOREA

When Da Hyeon's not taking photos:
She attends school and loves to read.

What's Your Vibe?

Here's how 18-year-old girls speak.

dope (*interjection, adj.*)
Good, or excellent. "It's like 'OK,' 'cool,'
'dope.' It's the chillest word."
Millie, AUSTRALIA

What's your vibe? (*idiom*)
Friendly greeting. "It's kind of like saying
'What's up?' or 'What you doing?'"
Maryclare, THE BRONX

dayum (*interjection*)
Expression of approval. Used "when
something cool happens."
Cinzia, GERMANY

Last last we go dey alright (*idiom*)
Optimistic saying immortalized by the
Nigerian rapper Kida Kudz. It means "at
the end of the day, we will be alright."
Victory, NIGERIA

B (*abbrev.*)
Term of endearment. "It is short for 'busy bee,' like honey."
Hélène, LOS ANGELES

peng (*interjection, adj.*)
"It just means 'good.'"
Ruby, U.K.

打扰了 (*pronounced* "dǎrǎole," *idiom*)
Embarrassed apology. "Translates to 'Sorry to bother,' which represents the sort of feeling you get when you go into the wrong room and are faced with an entire crowd of people."
Shenzhi, CHINA

헐 (*pronounced* "hull," *interjection*)
Expression of wonder or shock "which is used a lot when you're surprised."
Jung Eun, SOUTH KOREA

ne ukalaixis (*noun, pl.*)
Term of endearment among women. Translates to "my old ladies" in English. "That's usually what I call my sisters."
Obdulia, MEXICO

pressed (*adj.*)
Excitedly motivated. "To be hype about something and focused on it. 'I was pressed to get this care package in the mail.'"
Grace, WASHINGTON, D.C.

pinga (*noun, vulgar*)
"It means penis."
Thalia, CUBA

liar, dog, saala, and **mad** (*nouns, derogatory*)
Various insults. "I don't say much—only when I am angry, or when a stranger says something."
Mahak, INDIA

khawa (خاوة) (*pronounced* "khaa-wa," *verb*)
Affirmation. "It means 'whether you like it or not.'"
Faiza, WEST BANK

toп (*pronounced* "top," *adj.*)
Best, or top. "The highest quality of something: a top book, a top movie, a top person."
Alexandra, RUSSIA

יאללה (*pronounced* "ya-lah," *idiom, imperative*)
Expression used to motivate a sluggish companion, as in "Let's get going" or "Hurry up."
Lior, ISRAEL

GOAT (*acronym, noun*)
Greatest of all time. "They say Ronaldo is the GOAT in football. But I have been using it to identify myself. I feel like I am the greatest of all time."
Wanjiku, KENYA

Lori'anne Bemba
Montreal, Quebec

Lori'anne works at H&M and is enrolled in a pre-university program where she's studying international business. She has a brother and a twin sister.

PHOTOGRAPHED BY Adèle Foglia

What's your favorite app?
Instagram, because you can see what's going on in real time. I'm really curious, and sometimes I stalk a whole lot of people. So if someone talks about, like, his trip to Morocco in 2004, you pretend not to know about it but you actually know that he rode a camel and the whole thing. I like that you can see these moments in other people's lives.

How do you get around town?
Ninety percent of the time by metro. If not, by bike or by car.

Do you drive?

I got my learner's permit about a year ago, and since then I have been driving and I would like to advance, because I find it is a form of freedom. Not long ago, I went camping for three days with my friends—just us, alone, with no parents, and I was the one among my friends who drove. It was the first time we didn't have to depend on our parents. Well, you know, we had to depend on our parents to get the camping spot, and for the car because it was my mother's car . . . but it felt like mobile freedom.

So for you is driving related to becoming an adult?

Not becoming an adult, because I don't want to say that because I drive, I am an adult, but it does come with a responsibility—because the car is not like a game. Sometimes I am driving, and I say to myself—this is a bit freaky to say—but I say, like, "I could just do one bad maneuver and if there is a ditch in the side of the road, I could literally slide into it."

Lori'anne singing "God Is a Woman" by Ariana Grande while getting ready to go out.

In the car with her mom, Mone.

Who do you go to for advice?
I often ask my sister, or my mother, but I'm really stubborn and I like to have my own opinions. Often I'll think, "OK, I should be reasonable and follow their advice." But other times I'll be like, "I'll do it the way I want to."

Lori'anne training at the gym.

A night out
with friends.

When did you first feel like an adult?

It's when I started to pay my own bills: my phone, my Netflix, my gym—just basically all of my "necessities," and I put necessities in big quotation marks because a phone isn't a necessity. Like my teenage-ish student necessities. I mean, at 16 years old, I wasn't paying electricity—but I was thinking "OK, I'm going to set up [a savings account]," which I did.

Really, you have a savings account?

Yes, thanks to my mother, who is an accountant.

What do you think it means to be young?

I would say it's a period where you are looking for who you are, and you are still discovering who you are, what you want to do, what kind of person you want to be in this world.

Lori'anne with her sister and grandmother at a wedding; leaving the house for school.

Meet the Photographer

ADÈLE FOGLIA

21
Montreal,
QUEBEC

Something most people don't know about her:
"My ideal breakfast is a bowl of spaghetti with meatballs—don't get me started on toasts and cereals."

When Adèle's not taking photos:
She is in film school and is a part-time barista.

Wanjiku Muthoni Gakuru
Nairobi, Kenya

Wanjiku is studying urban planning at the University of Nairobi. In her spare time, she volunteers in classrooms in Kibera, the largest slum in Nairobi. She hopes to become an architect.

PHOTOGRAPHED BY Sarah Sunday Moses

Would you describe yourself as someone who loves food?
Oh yes. I love food. Everyone in our family loves eating. We use food as a channel to make us closer—and have a tighter bond. We eat, we talk, we check on each other, we celebrate if there was any birthday and also talk about life in general.

What kind of food do you love?
I love pilau (a dish of seasoned rice and often meat) with kachumbari (a vegetable salad). The truth is that I love pilau because of its ingredients. Pilau also looks yummy.

What do you like to do for fun?

I enjoy spending time with my friends talking about social issues, cracking jokes, and discussing controversial issues. Every weekend I am happy to see two of my friends. It has sort of become a routine because we don't get to see each other during the week.

Wanjiku, left, watching YouTube videos with a friend.

Buying vegetables in Kibera.

What do you do when you feel bored?

I like to listen to some music, particularly a music composition by one musician called Khalid. Khalid's music is a combination of hip-hop and pop. It's like a mixture. All his musical beats are of slow motion, which makes it easy to dance to. So when I am in a bad mood or when I am feeling sad, as soon as I listen to Khalid's music, I get to feel good. If I still feel unhappy or sad, I take a walk to get some fresh air.

172

What is your relationship with your parents like?
I am very blessed to have family members who are
very open. Since my childhood, I never got any
special treatment as the only child, as many would
have expected. This is because my dad knew for
sure that if he had overprotected me or treated me
in a special manner, no one else would teach me
about real life. There's a Swahili saying, "He who
is not taught by his or her mother will be taught
by the world." My dad never wanted anything like
that to occur to me when I grew up, so he took the
opportunity to mold me to become a responsible,
good-hearted girl who respected elders and knew how
to seize opportunities as they came.

What are your expectations now that you are 18?
I expect to grow to become a responsible woman. I would like to continue investing in other people's future; I would like to continue helping others. Even though I may not have money, I am blessed with other resources that I can use to help other people.

Meet the Photographer

SARAH SUNDAY MOSES

19
New Cush,
SUDAN

When Sarah Sunday's not taking photos:
"I'm usually doing poetry or pencil art."

Something most people don't know about her:
"My favorite food is ugali (a type of porridge) served with sukuma wiki (collard greens) and avocado."

Lior Danieli
Beersheba, Israel

Lior is a high school graduate who plays volleyball professionally. She was recently drafted into the military, which is mandatory for most Israelis.

PHOTOGRAPHED BY Noga Sieradzki

Can you recall the first time you felt like an adult?

I feel that in the past year I've become a more mature person, not necessarily in my behavior but around my independence. If I had to give a few examples, I'd say when I had exams for the military, when I started driving lessons, and also when I flew back alone with my grandmother and grandfather from Ukraine. All of those moments when you are under your own responsibility— it's a good feeling of independence.

Are you looking forward to serving in the military?

There's something a bit scary about starting military service. It's a new beginning, and it's not like starting a new school, it's joining an army—and that's the scary part—but there's also the anticipation of a new beginning. There's something stressful about new beginnings, but I've always enjoyed them.

Lior and her mother, Larissa, hold photos of themselves taken 25 years apart. Both played volleyball professionally.

Lior and her sister,
Sharon, in the
Mediterranean Sea.

What would you like to do 5 years from now?
It's hard to say, because I'm at a point right now where
I don't know where life will take me, even though I'm
sure I'll steer it. It depends what I end up doing in the
military, whether or not I'll be discharged in a few
years. I'm sure I'll go to a university. I want to spend
time with my family, to be a student, to go back to
sports, and to develop some kind of practice. I have
some dreams.

Like what?
Just like all these fantasies. I know I want to do things
beyond just studying, like dedicate time to my hobbies.
To live life freely, to do things I like doing.

Lior and her sister
on the beach in
Tel Aviv.

So you don't want to be someone who works for work?
It's important for me to work my way to where I want to be, to a good place in life.

What are some things that you don't know but want to learn?
Maybe sometime in the future I'll learn Italian; it's a really beautiful language. I'd also like to learn how to surf.

Meet the Photographer

NOGA SIERADZKI

20
Beersheba,
ISRAEL

Something most people don't know about her:
At her bat mitzvah, Noga partook in what's called the "Aliyah L'Torah"—which means she read a passage from the Torah aloud to the congregation. "In Israel most of the girls don't do it, so it's quite special here."

When Noga's not taking photos:
She serves as a soldier in the Israeli army.

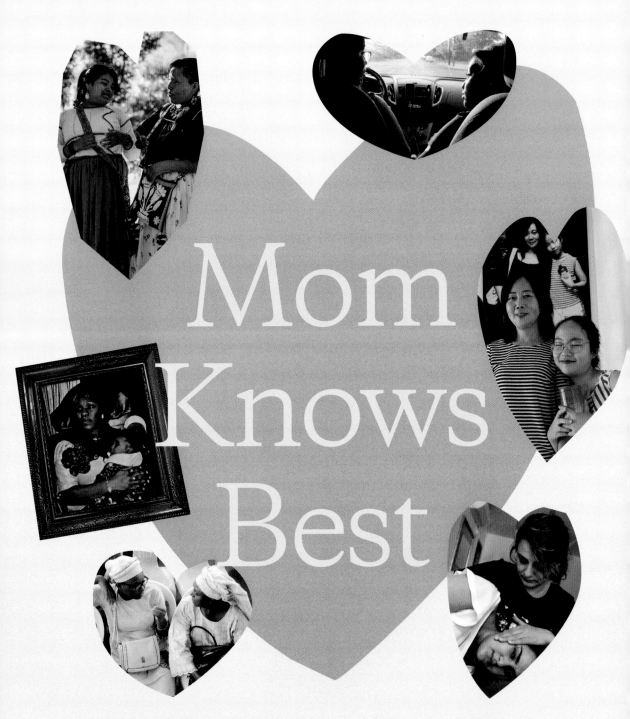

Mom Knows Best

Who do you go to for advice?
For these girls, it's their mothers.

"If I need advice on any issue, I turn to my mother. She knows a lot about worldly matters. She gives the right suggestions. She does not get angry or scold me if I do anything wrong. She softly advises me."

—Mahak, INDIA

"I go to my mom most often. She guides me to look for my way, instead of making a decision, and helps me think clearly so that I can do things by myself."

—Jung Eun, SOUTH KOREA

"To my mum. No matter what it is, to mum."

—Lior, ISRAEL

"My dad and mom. They've always let me be free and, as they say, if you let your child be free from the beginning, they won't turn out bad. I'd really like to raise my children like that in the future."

—Liana, IRAN

"Recently I watched *Gilmore Girls*, and I felt like it was talking about my life. That strong mother-daughter bond is exactly what I have. We navigate the world together."

—Hélène, CALIFORNIA

"My mom knows everything about me. We talk about all kinds of weird stuff. She is a friend, not only a mom."

—Anndrine, NORWAY

"I'd like to say my mum. I love my mum."

—Millie, AUSTRALIA

Cinzia Russo
Berlin, Germany

Cinzia is finishing up her final year of high school and hopes to become a psychologist. She spent most of her life in Italy and is of Italian and Nigerian descent.

PHOTOGRAPHED BY Constanze Josting

What is the farthest you've been from home?
Nigeria. I can't remember everything, but it's really different from here. I don't know how to explain it. Here everything is like a city and everything is just perfect, but there it's just people walking around without shoes and kids playing around with small games. One thing that I remember is that at night there's no light, so I was always a bit scared.

What place that you've never been would you most like to go?
Oh, this is easy. I love Asia and I would love to go to South Korea one day because I like the culture.

What do you do when you feel bored?

I usually watch videos or listen to music or read. Videos on Instagram—you know, just scrolling.

What's something you'd like to learn?

To play the piano. I tried learning when I was 6 years old, but I was really, really bad at it, so I just quit.

Looking at the world today, what's something that worries you?
I don't know, there are a lot of things. I'm afraid that in the future the new generation will forget about things like also going outside or reading a book because everything is just phone, phone, phone.

Cinzia at a
breakdance class.

What are you looking forward to about being 18?

Driving, I think. And in general, there are a lot of things that I can't do now, like go into a club. I'm not the party type, but maybe sometimes I would like to go with my friends. It's really weird, turning 18. I think the thing I look forward to the most is not needing my parents to sign everything. I could just sign it, and then it's like . . . I signed it, it's legal.

Cinzia, left, with friends Antonella and Can at a birthday party.

Cinzia, in black, sings in the church choir.

Meet the Photographer

CONSTANZE JOSTING

18
Berlin,
GERMANY

Something most people don't know about her:
As a child, she wanted to be a farmer or a dragon tamer. "There were no other careers that seemed worth considering."

When Constanze's not taking photos:
"I'm currently learning Arabic in my dad's home country, Palestine, and I also like spending time in nature and meeting new people."

Rawnaa Babunnji
Jeddah, Saudi Arabia

Rawnaa is in her first year of college and works part-time as a barista. She lives with her mother and siblings and has a cat named Christina.

PHOTOGRAPHED BY Lujain M. Sonbo

What do you want to be doing in 5 years?
I will have graduated from college. I would like to be working in my real job of being a pilot in the airline industry. This is my dream job.

How did you get interested in piloting?
I started watching some films and documentaries and reading a lot of articles about planes. I also have some friends who are working in the same field, and recently I started taking a few courses in flying. I love that I can be in the sky and fly. I can see the whole world.

What is something you'd like to learn?
Driving.

Women in Saudi Arabia were only recently granted the right to drive. Do you plan to get your driver's license?
Yes, I do; I am going to apply for driving classes in the coming months. What excites me and encourages me about getting my license is to be independent so I can go places, on trips by myself, which would be really nice and make me so happy. My older sisters have the driving license and they already started driving.

Rawnea at the coffee shop where she works.

Do you go driving with them?
I have—it's a refreshing feeling, honestly; seeing my sister drive and being able to go around with her is such an experience that I enjoy doing every time.

Where do you go?
To the café with friends or work sometimes. My mom and father have no problem with us jumping and going because they know where we go.

With Christina
the cat.

When did you first feel like a grown-up?
The first time I got a paycheck, around
a year ago. My first job was as an
assistant community manager in a
local coworking space. I got 3,000
ر.س. (Saudi riyal), or about $800. I felt
happy because this was the first step
in becoming financially independent.
And it fits right into my future plan to
become completely independent and live
on my own.

Meet the Photographer

LUJAIN M. SONBO

18
Jeddah,
SAUDI ARABIA

When Lujain's not taking photos:
She sews, does yoga, and hangs out with her six cats.

Something most people don't know about Lujain:
She speaks Turkish fluently.

Now it's your turn. What advice would you give your 18-year-old self?

Here's what Hillary Clinton, Gloria Steinem, and other strong women had to say.

"You won't have to wait for others to decide your life—not a husband and children and not convention. You will be able to decide your own life. Knowing that would have saved me so much time!"

–Gloria Steinem, in a high school yearbook photo from 1952

"Age is just a number. So often girls are told no. No, you can't do this or be this because society says you need to fulfill certain conditions. Well, to that I say: Prove them wrong."

–Amanda Nguyen, former NASA intern and Nobel Peace Prize nominee

"For a girl who likes to have a plan, you're going to have to take a lot of leaps of faith. But believe in yourself, you're doing great."

–Hillary Clinton, in in Park Ridge, Illinois, 1965

"Always tell people close to your heart that you love them. Say it often. Show it. You never know when they won't be around."

–Charo Henríquez, SAN JUAN, PUERTO RICO, 1992

"Women are powerful and can do whatever they want, but generally lip liner is not a good idea."

–Meena Harris, OAKLAND, CALIFORNIA

"Clearly, you're a weird kid with a different outlook and vision about life. That is perfectly okay."

–Alisha Vasudev, MUMBAI, INDIA, blaring Sugar Ray on her boombox on a school trip

"I know you feel like you're displaced, like you don't belong anywhere, but the truth is you belong to all the places you're from and all the places you'll go, and they all belong to you."

–Maya Salam, BEIRUT and MONTANA, 1998

"You don't need to wait for anyone to give you permission to be yourself. Let go of the people who won't accept you for who you are."

–Tiffany Yu, WASHINGTON, D.C., 2006

"Failure is inevitable. So just expect it and try not to fear it. Definitely don't be ashamed by it."

–Deborah Alejandra, ORANJESTAD, ARUBA, 1980

"If I could talk to this version of myself, I'd let her know that forgiveness and understanding is something she deserves. I would also tell her to call her parents more."

–Kimberly Drew, NORTHAMPTON, MASSACHUSETTS, 2009

"Your mind, even though it's filled with creativity and beautiful things, is also haunted by mental illness. I know it sucks and you wish it would just stop. But the fight never stops, and that's okay."

—Isabella Dias, Belém, BRAZIL, 2018

"Don't second-guess your decisions or abilities. Stop thinking about it and just do it. And also, wash your makeup off at night."

—Alexandra Tweten, Climax, MINNESOTA, 2005

"Stop worrying so much about 'doing it right.' And pastels are definitely not your thing, especially pink."

—Jodi Rudoren, NEWTON, MASSACHUSETTS, 1998

Share a photo of yourself at 18 with the hashtag #ThisIs18 on your favorite social platform. (Braces and bad hair welcome!)

What advice would you give to that girl in the photo?

About the Editors

They were 18 once too!

JESSICA BENNETT is an award-winning journalist who has spent her career focusing a gender lens on social issues and culture. She was the first-ever gender editor at *The New York Times* and is the author of *Feminist Fight Club: A Survival Manual for a Sexist Workplace,* which has been translated into 12 languages. She recently got to interview Liz Phair, one of Jessica's idols when she was 18.

SANDRA STEVENSON, right, is currently an assistant editor in the photography department of *The New York Times,* where she has worked for 13 years. She is a mom to an 18-year-old son and wife to a Frenchman.

ANYA STRZEMIEN is a deputy editor of *The New York Times* Styles section. Her first job in media was a zine she created at age 15 called *Love*.

SHARON ATTIA is a researcher and social media editor for *The New York Times* who recently graduated with a degree in photojournalism. When she was 18—not that long ago!—she had to physically flip her camera around to take a selfie.

With Thanks to Our Mentors

DANIEL BOETKER-SMITH is an educator, writer, curator, publisher, and photographer based in Melbourne.

OSSAIN RAGGI GONZALES is an artist and a professor living and working in Havana, Cuba.

MONA BOSHNAQ is a London-based photo editor for the *New York Times*.

CHANDLER GRIFFIN is a Los Angeles-based documentary filmmaker and media educator and the founder of Barefoot Workshops and cofounder of Blue Magnolia Films.

IMAN AL-DABBAGH is a documentary photographer and videographer in Saudi Arabia and California.

VINIT GUPTA is a documentary photographer based in New Delhi, India.

BARBARA DAVIDSON is a three-time Pulitzer Prize and Emmy award-winning photojournalist.

TANYA HABJOUQA is a Jordanian/Texan photographer and educator based in East Jerusalem.

JAMES ESTRIN joined the *New York Times* as a photographer in 1992 and is the coeditor of Lens, the *Times*'s photography blog.

INGE HELLAND is the founder and head of Bilder Nordic School of Photography, Scandinavia's largest photo school.

BIANCA FARROW is the education manager at the Bronx Documentary Center, a nonprofit gallery and educational space in the South Bronx.

HYUN SIL JUNG teaches photojournalism at the University of Photography Education for the blind.

GRISELDA SAN MARTIN is a Spanish documentary photographer who, for the past six years, has documented the U.S.-Mexico border.

BENEDICTE KURZEN is a French photographer who, for the past decade, has been covering conflicts and socioeconomic changes in Africa.

NEWSHA TAVAKOLIAN is a Magnum Photos photographer based in Tehran.

DAVID LEHMAN is the director of the Photo Start Foundation, which teaches life and business skills through photography to students in impoverished communities.

ANNIE TRITT began her career as a photojournalist at the age of 36 working in New York, following a career as a teacher and stay-at-home parent.

IAN WILLMS is a founding member of Boreal Collective and NAMARA Represents.

HEIDI LEVINE is an American freelance photojournalist based in Jerusalem.

MUYI XIAO is the visuals editor for ChinaFile, an online magazine about China published by the Asia Society's Center on U.S.-China Relations.

MISCO MUNGAI leads the Paza Program at Akili Dada, which works with female high school graduates to transition into university and beyond.

OKSANA YUSHKO is an award-winning photographer and visual artist currently focused on post-Soviet countries.

Shout-Outs

With huge thanks to our editors and collaborators at *The New York Times*, especially badass boss lady Jodi Rudoren. To Choire Sicha, who we will need to blackmail for his #thisis18 photo, and James Estrin, who was key in helping us identify photographers around the world. To Umi Syam, Bonnie Wertheim, and Francesca Donner: You rock. With additional thanks to Alex Ward, Steve Brown, and the many others who helped bring this project to life.

Dreaming About the Future

Here's where the girls see themselves in 5 years.

"I want to be studying psychology at university. I want to be moved out; I want to have my life in order."

–Millie, AUSTRALIA

"I hope I can do everything according to my family's wishes, with their blessings."

–Shama, BANGLADESH

"I would like to start a sustainable business venture."

–Wanjiku, KENYA

"I want to be studying and partake in politics."

–Anndrine, NORWAY

"I would like to be a teacher."

–Mahak, INDIA

"I'll probably be in my first year of medical school."

–Maryclare, THE BRONX, NEW YORK

"I want to play my instrument. I don't care about concerts or fame; I just want to play well."

–Liana, IRAN

"I want to spend time with my family, to be a student, to go back to sports, and to develop some kind of practice."

–Lior, ISRAEL

"I would like to go to Australia to learn how to do body painting professionally."

–Jung Eun, SOUTH KOREA

"I would love to see myself with my own house."

–Madison, MISSISSIPPI

"I hope that I'll be happy with what I'm doing and liking life as much as I do right now."

–Lori'anne, CANADA

"I intend to be working as a self-made woman."

–Victory, NIGERIA

"I would like to be working as a pilot. This is my dream job."

–Rawnaa, SAUDI ARABIA

"I dream a lot about having a family. Maybe I'll study theoretical physics. Maybe me and a friend will open a cartoon studio. Everything is possible."

–Alexandra, RUSSIA

"I would like to be a contributor with positive impact on the lives of the people around me."

–Faiza, WEST BANK

Follow This Is 18 online:
#ThisIs18 (Instagram)

Follow Jessica Bennett online:
@jessicabennett

Follow *The New York Times*—Gender
online: @nytgender

This Is 18

ENGLISH

这是18

CHINESE

Esto es 18

SPANISH

C'est 18

FRENCH

18 هذه/اذه

ARABIC

18살입니다

KOREAN